A TUNE A DAY

FOR CELLO.

BY C. PAUL HERFURTH.

BOOK ONE.

Exclusive Distributors:

Music Sales Limited
Distribution Centre, Newmarket Road,
Bury St Edmunds, Suffolk IP33 3YB, UK.

Music Sales Pty Limited
20 Resolution Drive, Caringbah, NSW 2229, Australia.

Order No. BM10082
ISBN 978-0-7119-1554-1

BOSTON MUSIC COMPANY.

PUPIL'S PRACTICE RECORD

	SEPT.					OCT.					NOV.					DEC.					JAN.				
	1	2	3	4	5	1	2	3	4	5	1	2	3	4	5	1	2	3	4	5	1	2	3	4	5
Monday																									
Tuesday																									
Wednesday																									
Thursday																									
Friday																									
Saturday																									

	FEB.					MAR.					APR.					MAY					JUNE				
	1	2	3	4	5	1	2	3	4	5	1	2	3	4	5	1	2	3	4	5	1	2	3	4	5
Monday																									
Tuesday																									
Wednesday																									
Thursday																									
Friday																									
Saturday																									

Always Record Practice Time in Minutes. All Practice Time Lost Must Be Made Up.

WEEKLY GRADE

NAME ....   ADDRESS ....

TEL. ....   SCHOOL ....   GRADE ....

	Sept.	Oct.	Nov.	Dec.	Jan.	Feb.	Mar.	Apr.	May	June	Tests
1st Week											
2nd Week											
3rd Week											
4th Week											

E—Excellent; G—Good; M—Medium, Distinctly Above Passing; L—Low, Doubtfully Passing; F—Very Poor, Failure.

FOREWORD TO TEACHERS

IN compiling this course the objective has intentionally been not to cover too much ground; but rather to concentrate on the acquisition of a thorough musical background and a solid foundation in good 'cello playing. These two requisites are inseparable.

A brief section is devoted to the simpler rudiments of music which should first be thoroughly understood. Another introductory section discusses the holding of the 'cello and bow, since, without the correct position of the left hand, and the proper drawing of the bow, good 'cello playing is impossible. With this in mind, considerable material has been given for the open strings before attempting the use of the fingers.

The accurate placing of each finger should be insisted upon.

Cultivate in the pupil the habit of careful listening.

The familiar hymns and folk-songs have been selected because of their melodic interest as pieces, and because, in addition, in each appears some technical point to be mastered.

The value of learning to count aloud from the very beginning cannot be over-estimated. Only in this way can a pupil sense rhythm. Rhythm, one of the most essential elements of music, and usually conspicuous by its absence in amateur ensemble playing, is emphasized throughout. For instance, Lesson 12 emphasizes an essential step in rhythmic development.

Many teachers do the thinking for their pupils, instead of helping them to think for themselves. Insisting upon the mastery of each point will not dull their interest.

What greater joy, whether it be child or adult, than to accomplish, achieve, and gain more power.

Lessons marked "Supplementary Material" may be given as a reward for well-prepared work.

Class teaching should be a combination of individual instruction and ensemble playing. At every lesson there should be individual playing so that all the necessary corrections can be made. Never allow pupils' mistakes to go unnoticed, since only in constant correction will they develop the habit of careful thinking and playing.

A decided advantage of group-teaching is that it provides experience in ensemble playing and gives every pupil the opportunity of listening to the others, of observing their mistakes, and of hearing the corrections.

For the best results each class should not be made up of more than six for a half-hour lesson, and twelve for an hour lesson. Irrespective of the numbers, the teacher must see to it that there is individual instruction as well as general directions to the class.

Classes should be regraded whenever necessary so as not to retard the progress of the brighter students, nor to discourage the slower ones. It also acts as an incentive for greater effort on the part of the pupils.

It is recommended that every student practice forty-five minutes a day. This course provides one lesson a week for a school year.

The eventual success of each pupil depends on the regular and careful home practice, according to directions.

If possible it would be well for the teacher to keep in touch with the parents.

Grateful acknowledgment is made by the author for the assistance of many teachers under whose direction this course has been used.

C. PAUL HERFURTH
Director of Instrumental Music
East Orange, N. J.

FOREWORD TO THE REVISED EDITION

Although the outstanding success of "A TUNE A DAY" in its original form for violin has far exceeded the author's expectations, its use in many school systems throughout this country, Canada and Australia has prompted the author to consult with a number of these teachers, to discuss the possibility of improvement.

Because the material has been subjected to the routine of actual classroom teaching, it has been constantly revised and improved in the light of this experience, until in its present form it represents a thoroughly workable course of study for string class teaching.

In this revised edition the author has eliminated certain exercises for which no immediate need was necessary, and has incorporated additional material in the form of new melodies, and secondary teacher parts.

The addition of a piano book to aid the pupils in ear-training and rhythm will greatly enhance the value of this course.

C. P. H.

RUDIMENTS OF MUSIC

Music is represented on paper by a combination of characters and signs, all of which it is necessary to learn in order to play the 'Cello intelligently.

Characters called notes are written upon and between five lines which is called the staff.

The character placed at the beginning of the staff is called the Bass or F clef.

The staff is divided by bars into measures as follows.

These measures, in turn, are equal in time value, according to the fractional numbers, (Time signature) placed at the beginning of each piece.

The time signature indicates the number of notes of equal value in each measure. The upper figure gives the number of beats or counts in a measure, and the lower figure indicates what kind of a note has one beat, such as $\frac{4}{4}$ or $\mathbf{C}$ equals four quarter notes or the equivalent half note and two quarters in each measure; $\frac{2}{4}$ equals 2 quarter notes; $\frac{4}{8}$ equals 4 eighth notes, etc.

There are different kinds of notes, each variety representing a certain time value as follows:

Whole Note equals, Two Half Notes, Four Quarter Notes, or Eight Eighth Notes.

The count for the above would be, four to the whole note: two to each half note, one to each quarter note and one to each group of two eighth notes.

The notes are named after the first seven letters of the alphabet, i. e., (a, b, c, d, e, f, g,) according to the line on or space in which they are placed.

The Bass or F clef which starts on the fourth line, establishes the note F on this line, from which the other lines and spaces are named as follows:

In addition, notes are written upon and between short lines above and below the staff. These lines are called leger lines.

Compass of the 'Cello in the first position, showing notes playable on each string used in this book.

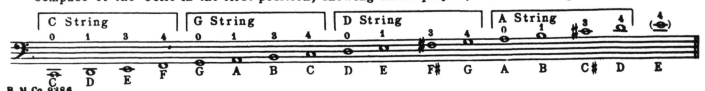

B. M. Co. 9386

Line Notes   Space Notes

Good   **B**oys   **D**eserve   **F**avors   **A**lso   **A**ll   **C**hildren   **E**njoy   **G**oodies

A rest indicates a pause, or silence for the value of the note after which it is named, such as

Whole Rest   **Half Rests**   **Quarter Rests**   **Eighth Rests**

THE 'CELLO

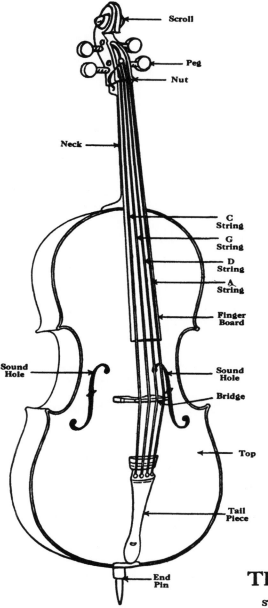

The end of a piece is indicated by a light and heavy line.

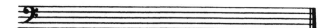

When a section or part of a piece is to be repeated, it will be shown by a double bar with two dots.

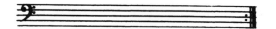

KEY SIGNATURES

The Sharps or Flats found after the Clef at the beginning of each line is called the Key Signature.

These Sharps or Flats effect all the notes of the same name throughout the piece, except when changed by a new Key Signature or temporarily by an accidental. An Accidental is a Sharp or Flat which does not belong to the Key Signature. An Accidental applies only to the measure in which it is placed.

SHARPS, FLATS, AND NATURALS

A Sharp (♯) raises the note to which it applies by one-half tone.

A Flat (♭) lowers the note to which it applies by one-half tone.

A Natural (♮) takes away the effect of a sharp or flat and restores the note to its original pitch.

THE BOW

HOLDING THE 'CELLO

Fig. I
Rest Position

SIT rather well forward on the chair so that your body is in a natural erect position. Hold the 'cello firmly between the knees (just above its greatest width) so that the right knee is against the right side, and the left knee is against the left side. The right, upper back edge of the 'cello should rest against your chest.

The instrument should be adjusted as to height by the tail-pin so that the C string peg (lower right) is on a level with your left ear.

POSITION OF THE LEFT HAND AND THUMB

Fig. II

WITH your left hand in a half closed position, place the ball of your thumb against the back of the neck about three and one half (3½) inches down. Fingers curved over the fingerboard. The first finger approximately three (3) inches down from the nut; the second and third fingers should be curved so that their tips may be pressed firmly upon the strings. The fourth or little finger is also slightly curved. Firmness of left hand fingers (playing with the fingertips) is of the utmost importance for good tone production.

HOLDING THE BOW

Take the bow in the left hand, and hold at the extreme end below the frog, in such a position that the hair is facing up and the tip of the bow is pointing away from you (Fig. III). (1) Place the TIP of the thumb (right hand) slightly curved at the joint, against the stick so that it touches the raised part of the frog on the stick (Fig. III and IV). (2) Allow the middle finger to curve around the stick at the first joint (from the tip) opposite the thumb. (3) Place the third, or ring finger, next to the middle finger so that it curves around the stick at the first joint, and rests against the side of the frog. (4) Allow the first finger to rest on the stick in the first joint. (5) The *tip* of the little finger rests on the stick in a natural position. Release the left hand. The fingers should be close together (Fig. V and VI).

The bow is controlled by the first three fingers and the thumb.

The bow hair for playing should be tightened so that it is about a quarter of an inch away from the stick at the center of the bow. Always loosen the hair when not playing.

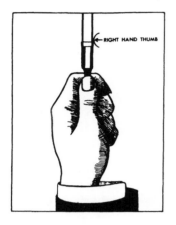

Fig. III

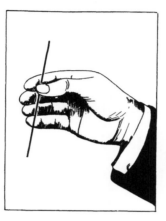

Fig. IV
Showing position of bow stick in relation to fingers

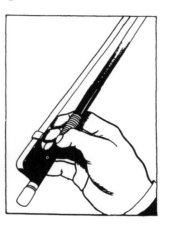

Fig. V

Fig. VI

SILENT EXERCISES FOR THE BOW

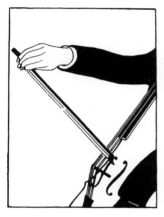

Fig. VII
Position of bow while playing at the tip

With the 'cello in position, place the bow on the **A** string at different points, i.e., at the middle, tip, and frog. At each point hold the bow perfectly still for 2 minutes. Take notice of the position of arm, wrist, etc. as follows. The bow must always be at right angles to the strings, i.e., parallel with the bridge, and midway between the finger-board and bridge. When the bow is at the point, the wrist should be sunk in (very slightly) and when at the frog, should be curved up (not too much). The hand is always in the same relative position to the bow. Do not allow the fingers to move on the bow stick. When placing the bow on the strings, the stick is turned slightly towards the fingerboard, so that only the edge of the hair touches the strings. This rule varies according to the dynamic effect desired. Practice this on all strings.

Fig. VIII
Position of bow while playing at the frog

Notice that the elbow is slightly higher when playing on the **A** and **D** strings, but never should the elbow be higher than the hand. Raise the hand to the level of the string desired, keeping the elbow entirely relaxed. Any exertion of the upper arm muscles is very harmful to a good tone (Fig. VII and VIII).

SIGNS AND ABBREVIATIONS FOR BOWING

⊓ means Down Bow   **W.B.** means Whole Bow
V means Up Bow   **M.H.** means Middle half of Bow

TUNING YOUR 'CELLO

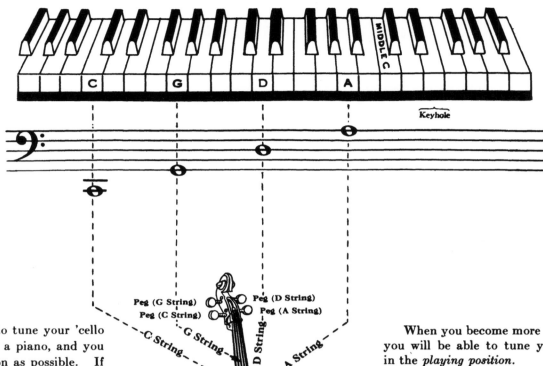

IT is quite easy to tune your 'cello with the aid of a piano, and you should learn as soon as possible. If no piano is available use a 'cello pitch-pipe.

DIRECTIONS

Hold the 'cello by the larger end between the knees, the strings toward you. Strike the note **A** on the piano (see diagram), or blow it on the pitch-pipe. With the thumb of the left hand pick the **A** string to compare it with the piano. If the string sounds lower (flat) the pitch of the string must be raised by turning the **A** peg away from you with the right hand. Turn the peg slowly while picking the string with the left thumb until it sounds in unison with the piano or pitch-pipe. If the string sounds higher (sharp) than the piano it must be lowered by turning the peg slowly toward you until the pitch of the string is the same as the piano. Tune the **D** string, in the same manner as the **A** string.

To tune the **G** and **C** strings, reverse the hands, the left hand turning the pegs while plucking the strings with the thumb of the right hand.

While turning the pegs always press them into the holes so that they will stay in position when you take your hand away.

Tune the strings in the following order, **A - D - G - C.**

When you become more advanced you will be able to tune your 'cello in the *playing position.*

TAKE CARE OF YOUR 'CELLO

Your 'cello will not sound its best, nor will your learning to play it be as easy unless everything pertaining to the instrument is kept in perfect condition.

If your 'cello is not a new one it should be taken to an instrument repairer for all necessary adjustments. Your teacher will tell you what is needed to put your 'cello in good playing condition.

Always keep your 'cello in the case when not practicing. NEVER loosen the strings on your 'cello but ALWAYS loosen the hairs on the bow when not playing. Rosin the bow-hair a little each day. Never allow rosin to collect on the 'cello or on the bowstick; ALWAYS keep them clean.

Take a pride in the way your 'cello looks as well as in how it sounds. Use good strings, and ALWAYS have an extra set in your 'cello bag.

When not practicing, stand the 'cello in a corner with the strings turned toward the wall.

CARRYING YOUR 'CELLO

Carry the 'cello at your side in an upright position with the strings toward your body. (Bridge forward.)

A strap is provided on the side of the bag for your hand.

FOREWORD FOR OPTIONAL LESSONS ONE THROUGH FIVE

Although the outstanding success of "A TUNE A DAY" in its present form has far exceeded the author's expectations, its use in many school systems throughout this country, Canada, and Australia has prompted the author to consult with a number of these teachers, to discuss the use of the quarter note approach.

The thinking of string teachers seems to be about equally divided between the whole note and the quarter note approach for beginning string instrument students.

In order to make the "TUNE A DAY" string class method more valuable to those teachers who prefer the quarter note approach, the author has compiled optional material for the first five lessons with this objective in mind. These optional lessons appear in the violin, viola, 'cello, and bass books, thus providing for the teaching of these instruments in one group through the class procedure.

In order to simplify the learning of holding the instrument and bow at the same time, the first lesson uses the pizzicato approach through employing open string letter names only, thus eliminating the holding of the bow and the reading of pitch names on the staff.

With this approach in 2/4 rhythm the beginner is better able to think and feel the pulsation of this marching rhythm.

The whole and half note approach remains the same as before, starting with the regular Lesson One (1) on Page 1 for those teachers who prefer this procedure.

The author believes that, with these first five optional lessons included in the series of "A TUNE A DAY", it now covers the needs of all discriminating string teachers.

C. PAUL HERFURTH.

LESSON 1
(OPTIONAL)

The Open Strings Pizzicato

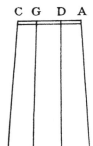

C G D A

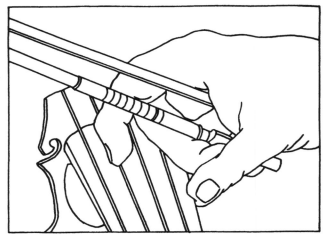

Pizzicato (Pizz.) = Plucking the strings. After learning the left hand position in holding the 'Cello (page VI), the names and positions of the open strings should be understood. See diagram showing pizz. position as follows: Place the tip of the thumb (right hand) against the upper edge of the fingerboard (about four inches from the lower end) under the C string and pluck the strings with the first finger.

Additional exercises for open strings G, D, A, Pizz., may be written on the blackboard.

REPEAT QUARTER
SIGN REST

① **Pizz.** A - A | A - A | D - D | D - D | A - A | A - A | D - D | D - D .‖ D - 𝄿 ‖
Count: 1 - 2 | 1 - 2 | 1 - 2 | 1 - 2 | 1 - 2 | 1 - 2 | 1 - 2 | 1 - 2 ‖ 1 - 2 ‖

② **Pizz.** D - D | D - D | G - G | G - G | D - D | D - D | G - G | G - G ‖ G - 𝄿 ‖
Count: 1 - 2 | 1 - 2 | 1 - 2 | 1 - 2 | 1 - 2 | 1 - 2 | 1 - 2 | 1 - 2 ‖ 1 - 2 ‖

③ **Pizz.** A - A | D - D | A - A | D - D | A - A | D - D | A - A | D - D .‖ D - 𝄿 ‖
Count: 1 - 2 | 1 - 2 | 1 - 2 | 1 - 2 | 1 - 2 | 1 - 2 | 1 - 2 | 1 - 2 ‖ 1 - 2 ‖

④ **Pizz.** D - D | G - G | D - D | G - G | D - D | G - G | D - D | G - G ‖ G - 𝄿 ‖
Count: 1 - 2 | 1 - 2 | 1 - 2 | 1 - 2 | 1 - 2 | 1 - 2 | 1 - 2 | 1 - 2 ‖ 1 - 2 ‖

⑤ **Pizz.** D - A | D - G | D - A | D - G | D - A | D - G | D - A | D - G .‖ G - 𝄿 ‖
Count: 1 - 2 | 1 - 2 | 1 - 2 | 1 - 2 | 1 - 2 | 1 - 2 | 1 - 2 | 1 - 2 ‖ 1 - 2 ‖

NOT IN UNISON

⑥ **Pizz.** A - A | A - A | A - A | A - A | A - D | A - A | A - D | A - A ‖ A - 𝄿 ‖
Count: 1 - 2 | 1 - 2 | 1 - 2 | 1 - 2 | 1 - 2 | 1 - 2 | 1 - 2 | 1 - 2 ‖ 1 - 2 ‖

NOT IN UNISON

⑦ **Pizz.** G - G | C - C | G - G | C - C | G - C | G - D | G - C | G - D ‖ G - 𝄿 ‖
Count: 1 - 2 | 1 - 2 | 1 - 2 | 1 - 2 | 1 - 2 | 1 - 2 | 1 - 2 | 1 - 2 ‖ 1 - 2 ‖

Ten Little Indians

Pizz. | **2** D - D | D - D | A - A | A - A | D - D | D - D | A - A | D - D ‖
Count: | **4** 1 - 2 | 1 - 2 | 1 - 2 | 1 - 2 | 1 - 2 | 1 - 2 | 1 - 2 | 1 - 2 ‖

American Folk-Tune

Piano

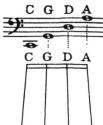

LESSON 2*
(OPTIONAL)
Holding and Drawing the Bow

After acquiring the feeling for holding the bow correctly (P. VII)(in the beginning this can be done much easier with a pencil) try playing on the open strings.* The right arm must be completely relaxed to permit the bow to be drawn freely.

Silent bow exercises: With the left hand and arm holding an imaginary 'Cello move the right hand and arm down and up as in actual playing until complete relaxation has been accomplished. When using the bow avoid all tension in the bow arm. ⊓ = Down Bow. ∨ = Up Bow.

Study the names of the open strings in relation to the notes as written on the staff,(see diagram above).You are now playing quarter notes (one count to each note) COUNT ALOUD.

---

*Procedure for this lesson.(1) Recite letter names in rhythm.(2) Play pizz. counting one-two.(3) Play using bow. The bow must be held firmly with the fingers of the right hand. Use the middle two-thirds of the bow and play with a bold firm stroke. Be careful of any tension in the bow arm.

** Piano Acc. Teacher's Manual, Page 6

LESSON 3
(OPTIONAL)
Continuation of Open String Quarter Notes
(One Count Each)

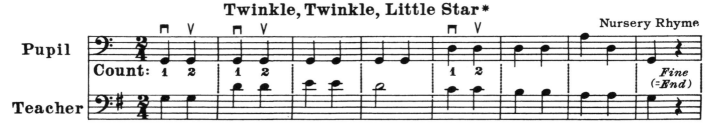

Twinkle, Twinkle, Little Star*

Nursery Rhyme

Oats and Beans

Old English

* Piano Acc. Teacher's Manual, Page 9

Home work: Write letter names above notes on this page.

LESSON 4
(OPTIONAL)

Half Notes - Two Counts Each

A half note is equal to two quarter notes tied. When two notes on the same degree of the staff (line or space) are tied by a slur ⌣ , they are to be played as one note.

USE A WHOLE BOW (W.B.) (FROG TO TIP, TIP TO FROG)

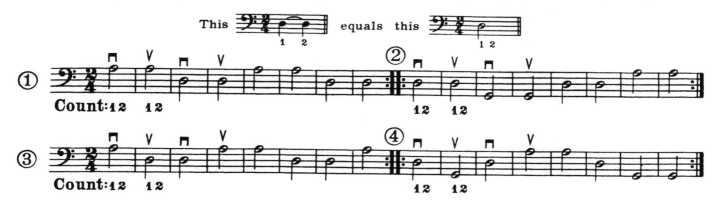

Introducing Four-Four (4/4) Time

Two measures of two-four time equal one measure of four-four time. The count for each measure now becomes one-two-three-four. One-two for the first half note, and three-four for the second half note.

* Piano Acc. Teacher's Manual, Page 4
** " " " " 5
*** " " " " 9

LESSON 5
(OPTIONAL)

Whole Notes - Four Counts Each

Draw the bow with an equality of motion in a straight line parallel with the bridge. Learn to save the bow, i.e., a fault that is very prevalent is the starting of the bow at a too rapid pace, whereby the greater part of the bow is used up before half the time value of the note has expired. Whole notes four counts, half notes two counts.

(Always count aloud and give each note its full value.) USE A WHOLE BOW (W.B.)

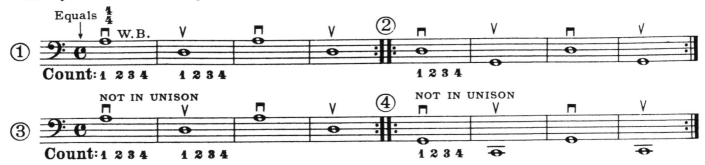

Whole Notes and Half Notes

DRAW THE BOW TWICE AS FAST FOR THE HALF NOTES AS FOR THE WHOLE NOTES.

Whole, Half, and Quarter Notes

Folk Song

Simplified piano accompaniments to all the exercises, scales and pieces in this book will be found in the Piano Accompaniment Book for home practice or in the Teacher's Manual. Accompaniments naturally stimulate practice thereby making progress more rapid when these accompaniment books are used.

A TUNE A DAY

LESSON 1
The Open Strings

Hold the bow firmly upon the strings while counting the rests. Draw the bow with an equality of motion in a straight line parallel with the bridge. Learn to save the bow, i.e., a fault that is very prevalent is the starting of the bow at a too rapid pace, whereby the greater part of the bow is used up before half the time value of the note has expired.

On the Cello

On the staff

The Open A-String

Whole notes four counts, half notes two counts. Use whole bow for each note, drawing the bow a little faster for the half notes than for the whole notes. ⊓ = Down bow, V = Up bow, W. B. = Whole bow.

Always count aloud and give each note its full value.

Au clair de la lune
French Folk-Song

Copyright 1937, by The Boston Music Co.

LESSON 2
The Open D-String

Whole notes four counts, half notes two counts. *Count aloud.*

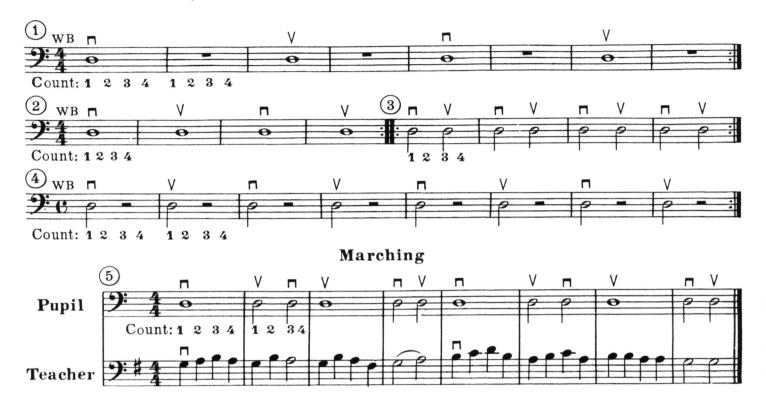

The Open A- and D-Strings

In crossing strings do not lift the bow off the string. Hold the bow firmly upon the string while raising or lowering the hand.

LESSON 3
Quarter Notes and Quarter Rests

1 count, use middle half of bow. Use whole bow for whole and half notes. Give quarter notes full value.

$\frac{2}{4}$ TIME MEANS { Two counts to a measure.
Quarter notes get one count.

Baa! Baa! Black Sheep

Nursery Rhyme

Hop, Hop, Hop!

German Folk-song

4

LESSON 4
The Open C-String
('Cello and Viola only)
(Piano accompaniments for Lesson 4 should be transposed)

Ten Little Indians
American Folk-tune

Oats and Beans
Old English

*A Riddle
German Folk-song

*By permission of Silver, Burdett & Co. owners of the copyright. From Book one, "The Progressive Music Series".

LESSON 5
The Open G-String

Twinkle, Twinkle, Little Star

The Four Open Strings
(Cello and Viola only)

Home work: Write **4** lines of open string notes, marking the name of each. Divide into measures, using whole, half and quarter notes. Mark time signature.

LESSON 6
The Eighth Note

To be played with a loose wrist and most generally with the middle part of the bow. Play slowly at first, gradually increasing the speed until you can play quite fast. *Count aloud.* Be careful not to cut the up bow stroke too short. Use the same amount of bow for notes of equal value.

Gaily The Troubadour

Thomas H. Bayly

Lightly Row

German Folk-tune

Home work: Write **4** lines of open string notes dividing into measures, using half, quarter and eighth notes in **4/4** and **2/4** time. Mark time signature.

Note: All manuscript pages are to be used for home-work according to instructions

TEST-QUESTIONS THROUGH LESSON 6

Questions from this, and following test-sheets, will be given as a check on your home-study of preceding lessons.

Remember: The more you know and understand about the signs and symbols used in music-writing, the easier it will be for you to learn how to play well.

(1) This ▯▯▯▯ is called?. . . . .

(2) This symbol 𝄢 is called?. . . . .

(3) The staff is divided by bar-lines into?. . . . .

(4) Fractions at the beginning of music are called?. . . . . signatures

(5) This 𝄢 is a . . . . note, and has . . . . counts?

(6) These 𝄢 are . . . . notes and have . . . . counts each?

(7) These 𝄢 are . . . . notes and have . . . . count each?

(8) These 𝄢 are . . . . notes and have . . . . count each?

(9) Lines and spaces are named after the first . . . . letters of the alphabet?

(10) This 𝄢 is a . . . . rest?

(11) These 𝄢 are . . . . rest?

(12) These 𝄢 are . . . . rest?

(13) This (♯) is a?. . . . .

(14) This (♭) is a?. . . . .

(15) How does a sharp affect a note?. . . . .

(16) How does a flat affect a note?. . . . .

(17) Name the open strings?. . . . .

(18) Write (notate) the open strings? 𝄢▯▯▯▯

(19) This sign ⊓ means?. . . . .

(20) This sign V means?. . . . .

First, second and third fingers must be perpendicular from the first joint to the tip when pressing on the strings. Keep the fingers over the strings. Do not allow the little finger to curl under the neck. Listen carefully that you play exactly in tune and give each note the proper time value.

First Finger B on the A-String
Whole tone from A to B

The 'Cello fingerboard as you see it from the playing position.

Little A and B March

Pupil

Teacher

First Finger E on the D-String
Whole tone from D to E

Little D and E March

Pupil

Teacher

Home work: Write 4 lines of the notes thus far studied, marking name of each, and finger used. Divide into measures using whole, half, and quarter notes; mark time signature.

Optional Material for Lessons 7 & 8

Now The Day is Over

J. Barnby

LESSON 8
First Finger B, third Finger C♯ on A-String
Whole tone A to B. Whole tone B to C♯
Key of A Major, F♯-C♯-G♯

First Finger E, third Finger F♯ on D-String
Whole tone D to E. Whole tone E to F♯
Key of D Major, F♯-C♯

Home work: Write 4 lines of notes as before, adding the two new notes in this lesson.

Write and study the key signatures of D and A Major.

✱ When two notes on the same degree of the staff are tied by a slur ⌢ , they are to be played as one note.

SUPPLEMENTARY MATERIAL

HARMONIZATION FOR LESSON VIII
Quartet for four 'Cellos

LESSON 9
On the A-String

First finger B, third finger C♯, fourth finger D
Whole Tone A to B, Whole Tone B to C♯, Half Tone C♯ to D
Key of A Major (F♯-C♯-G♯)

Learn to keep the fingers on the strings whenever possible. Rule: Never lift a finger unless obliged to. Press the fingers firmly upon the strings, but do not allow the hand to become cramped. Listen carefully to play in tune and always count. It is not music where there is no time or rhythm. *Have you a good position?*

This sign ‸ indicates half step, fingers close together.

On the D String

First finger E, third finger F♯, fourth finger G
Whole Tone D to E, Whole Tone E to F♯, Half Tone F♯ to G
Key of D Major (F♯-C♯)

Home work: Write 4 lines of notes thus far studied as before

Note: All manuscript pages are to be used for home-work according to instructions

LESSON 10
Slurred Notes(*legato)

This sign (⌢ slur) when placed above or below two or more notes indicates that they are to be played with one bow. Great care must be given to the *equal division* of the bow.

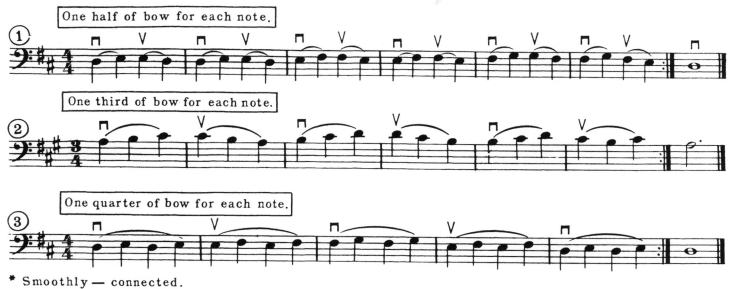

* Smoothly — connected.

The Scale

A scale is a succession of tones from a given note to its octave, 8 notes higher. The form on which all major scales are modeled is as follows:

The Natural, or C Major Scale

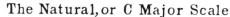
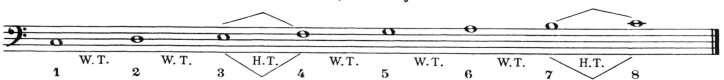

The ascending progression is: two whole tones, one half tone, three whole tones, one half tone. The half tones come between the numbers 3-4, 7-8.

The D Major Scale — four tones on the D string; four tones on the A string.

Play the following scale and arpeggio with different bowings as indicated; also play, slurring four notes to one bow. Use plenty of bow. Play slowly at first using whole bow for each note.

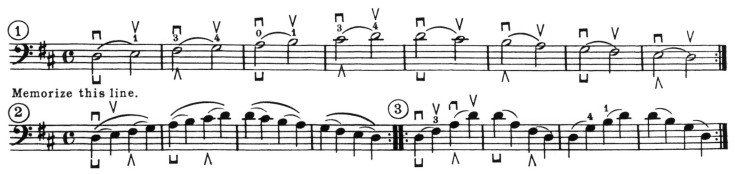

Memorize this line.

Home work: Write the D Major scale 4 times, marking half steps. Use key signature, and place a sharp before the notes affected.

LESSON 11
Up and Down the Ladder of D

* Fido and His Master
Duet

E. B. Birge

Reuben and Rachel
Duet

American Tune

German Folk Song

*Katydid

Bohemian Folk - song

*Polly's Bonnet

French Folk-song

* By permission of Silver, Burdett & Co. owners of the copyright. From Book one,"The Progressive Music Series."

LESSON 12
The Dotted Half Note and the Dotted Quarter Note

A dot is equal to one half the value of the note it follows. A dotted half note equals 3 beats, a dotted quarter note equals **1½** beats. Use the same amount of bow for the quarter note as for the half note.

Rhythm Drills

Play the model as written. Repeat, using each variation below until the rhythm is memorized.

Drill: Count aloud each variation while clapping the hands once for each note.   Repeat several times, then play on the open strings.

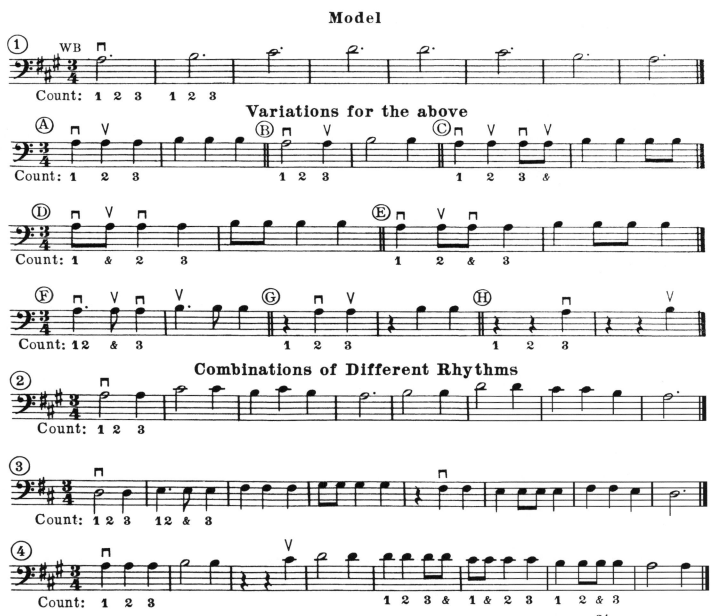

Home work: Write **4** lines of notes thus far studied, using different groupings of notes in $3/4$ time.

LESSON 13

My First Solo Pieces
(To be memorized)

Little Waltz in G

C. P. H.

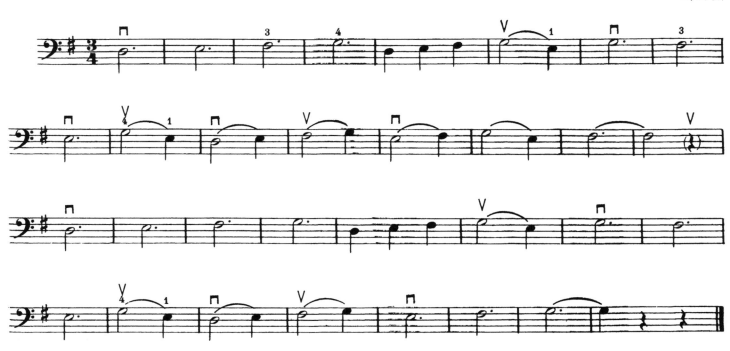

In A Garden

C. P. H.

LESSON 14
Using the D Major Scale

French Folk Song

French Folk Song

Joy to the World

Joy to the World

Beneath Thy Guiding Hand

TEST-QUESTIONS THROUGH LESSON 14

(1) This sign :‖: means?. . . . .

(2) This sign ⎯⎯⎯ means?. . . . .

(3) Name the following lines and spaces of the staff?

1st space.	2nd space . . . .
4th line.	1st line . . . .
3rd space.	2nd line . . . .
3rd line.	1st space below the staff. . . . .
4th space.	2nd line below the staff. . . . .

(4) The key of 2 sharps is?. . . . .

(5) The key of 3 sharps is?. . . . .

(6) This note 𝄢 has . . . . counts?

(7) This note 𝄢 3/4 has . . . . counts?

(8) Which finger should be used for the following notes?

C♯ on the A string	B on the A string . . . .
E on the D string	G on the D string . . . .
D on the A string	F♯ on the D string . . . .

(9) What note is played with the following fingers?

1st finger on the D string	4th finger on the A string . . . .
3rd finger on the A string	3rd finger on the D string . . . .
4th finger on the D string	1st finger on the A string . . . . . .

(10) Divide the following measures?

(11) Write (notate) the key-signatures of D and A Major?

(12) This sign ⌣ connecting two or more notes means?

(13) What is a scale?. . . . .

(14) Write and spell the D major scale?

(15) How many D's can you play?. . . . . E's . . . . G's . . . .

(16) Mark the count under the following?

(17) Play the D Major scale and arpeggio from memory. . . . .

(18) What is this 𝄢 called?. . . . .

LESSON 15

Detached Notes in One Bow

Semi-Staccato

A dot placed above or below two or more notes connected by a slur indicates that the notes are to be played in one bow with a short pause between each note. The bow is simply stopped and then started again. The bow, however, must not be lifted from the strings. A slight pinching of the stick at the beginning of each note will produce the desired effect.

Written   Played   Written   Played

Holy, Holy, Holy

Dykes

Theme from Second Symphony

HAYDN
Adapted

LESSON 16
Second Position

The second position is established by moving the left hand one tone higher on the fingerboard. In moving from one position to another the thumb always remains in the same relative position to the fingers, i.e. (opposite the second finger). Practice sliding from B to C♯ on the A string and from E to F♯ on the D string.

Old English Song
(Duet)

Lightly Row
(Duet)

The Cuckoo

LESSON 17
The Up-Beat

Many pieces begin with an incomplete measure, usually starting with the last beat or fraction thereof. This is called the up-beat and is generally played with an up bow. The ending always completes the measure of the up-beat. Follow the bowings carefully.

Two German Folk Songs
Harmonization

Away in a Manger
(Flow Gently, Sweet Afton)   Spilman

Away in a Manger

The First Noël
Christmas Carol

Blue Bells of Scotland
Old Scotch Air

German Folk Song

* Hold —— A short curved line drawn over a dot, prolongs the time of the note.

LESSON 18

Hymns and Folk Songs embracing the different kinds of notes and bowings thus far studied. Review the written work at the top of each page. Play the bowing and fingering as marked.

Old Black Joe
Stephen Foster

Old Black Joe

While Shepherds Watched Their Flocks
Arr. from Handel

Massa's in the Cold, Cold Ground
Stephen Foster

Gaily the Troubadour
Bayly

LESSON 19
Four tones on the C-String
('Cello and Viola only)
Open C to D Whole tone, D to E Whole tone,
E to F Half tone.
Key of C Major

(Piano accompaniments for Lesson 19 should be transposed.)

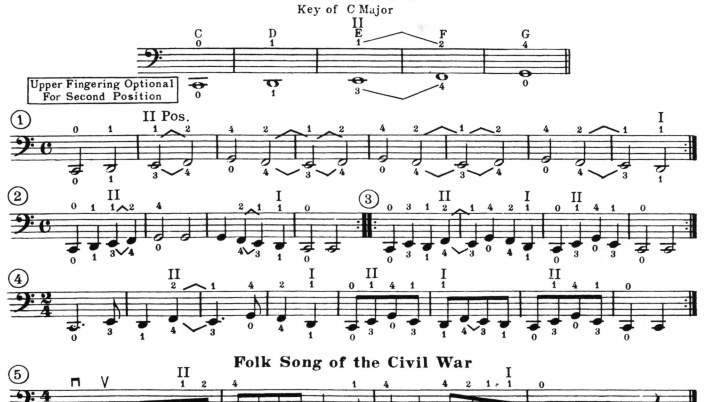

Folk Song of the Civil War

Scale of C Major
Half tones E to F, B to C

Use different bowings as indicated.

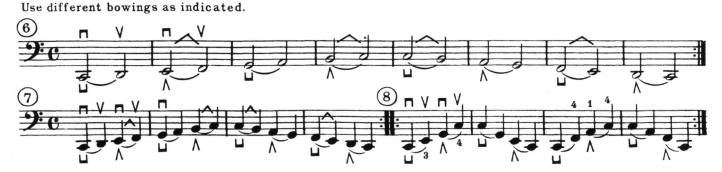

Auld Lang Syne
Scotch Folk-song

Home work: Write 4 lines of notes, using new notes on the C string. Mark name below and finger used above. Write C Major scale 5 times marking the same as the D Major. Study new key signatures.

B.M. Co. 9386

LESSON 20
Five tones on the G-String
Open G to A whole tone, A to B whole tone, B to C half tone, C to D whole tone.

Oats and Beans

Scale of G Major
One sharp, F♯. Half tones B to C, F♯ to G
Play the following scales and arpeggio with different bowings as indicated.

Old Folks at Home

Stephen Foster

MELODY

Old Folks at Home

Stephen Foster

ENSEMBLE

Home work: Write 4 lines of notes on the G string as before, also scale of G Major 4 times. **Mark half steps.**

LESSON 21

Review of the different keys, rhythms, and bowings thus far studied.

Annie Laurie

Scotch Air

Old Melody

Largo From New World Symphony
(MASSA DEAR)

Dvořak

Hymn

Henry Smart

Ensemble Playing

Pieces arranged for trio (*three parts*) and quartet (*four parts*) are given for your training in ensemble (*together*) playing, and also to prepare you for your place in the school orchestra. Tunes that you have played before in this book were selected so that you could hear the melody while playing a secondary part. Listen carefully to ALL the parts so that you keep in time and in tune(*harmony*) with them. Learn to play each part equally well so that you can take turns with the other members of your class in playing the different parts.

Twinkle, Twinkle, Little Star
(Trio for Three 'Cellos)

Arr. by C.P.H.

Teacher, advanced student or violin class may play melody

Pupil

Pupil

Twinkle, Twinkle, Little Star
Optional part for String Quartet

LESSON 23

Lightly Row
Trio for Three 'Cellos

Arr. C. P. H.

Teacher, advanced student, or violin class may play melody

Pupil

Pupil

Lightly Row
Optional part for String Quartet

German Folk Song
(Trio)

Arr. C. P. H.

Pupil

Pupil

Pupil

LESSON 24

Old Folks at Home
(Quartet for Four 'Cellos)

STEPHEN FOSTER
Arr. C. P. H.

LESSON 25

Old Black Joe
(Quartet for Four 'Cellos)

STEPHEN FOSTER
Arr. C. P. H.

TEST-QUESTIONS THROUGH LESSON 25

(1) This sign ⌢ means? : . . . .

(2) This 𝄾 is an . . . . rest?

(3) This sign : ⌒ : placed above or below two or more notes means? . . . .

(4) Finger the following?

(5) Bow the following?

(6) Mark the count under the following?

(7) Name the four tones on the C string? . . . .

(8) What is the signature of C Major? . . . .

(9) Write (notate) and spell the scale of C Major?

(10) Name the four tones on the G string? . . . .

(11) What is the signature of G Major? . . . .

(12) Write and spell the G Major scale?

(13) Finger the following?

(14) Finger the following?

(15) Write the following notes.

4th finger on the D string

3rd finger on the C string

1st finger on the G string

4th finger on the A string

4th finger on the G string

1st finger on the C string

3rd finger on the G string

3rd finger on the A string

1st finger on the A string

3rd finger on the D string

(16) Write the signatures of G—D—A and C major.

(17) How many of the following notes can you play?   C....B....G....A....E....

(18) Write (notate) your answers to No. 17.

(19) Music written for three instruments is called? . . . .

(20) Music written for four instruments is called? . . . .